$26.65   11/12 B&T

Exercise!

STAMINA

Get Stronger and Play Longer!

Ellen Labrecque

Heinemann
LIBRARY
Chicago, Illinois

www.capstonepub.com
Visit our website to find out
more information about
Heinemann-Raintree books.

To order:

☎ Phone 800-747-4992
💻 Visit www.capstonepub.com
to browse our catalog and order online.

© 2013 Heinemann Library
an imprint of Capstone Global Library, LLC
Chicago, Illinois

Edited by Rebecca Rissman, Daniel Nunn,
and Sian Smith
Designed by Steve Mead
Picture research by Ruth Blair
Production by Victoria Fitzgerald
Originated by Capstone Global Library Ltd
Printed and bound in China by Leo Paper
Products Ltd

16 15 14 13 12
10 9 8 7 6 5 4 3 2 1

Library of Congress Cataloging-in-Publication Data
Labrecque, Ellen.
  Stamina : get stronger and play longer! / Ellen
Labrecque.
    p. cm.—(Exercise!)
  Includes bibliographical references and index.
  ISBN 978-1-4329-6733-8 (hb)—ISBN 978-1-4329-6740-6
(pb) 1. Exercise. 2. Physical fitness. I. Title.
  GV461.L238 2012
  613.7'1—dc23   2011041387

Acknowledgments
We would like to thank the following for permission to
reproduce photographs: © Capstone Publishers pp. 15,
17, 21 (Karon Dubke); Corbis pp. 23 (© Bloomimage),
23 (© Juice Images), 25 (© Howard Kingsnorth/
cultura), 28 (© Stephane Mantey/TempSport); Getty
Images pp. 19 (Stephen Simpson); Shutterstock pp.
5 (© greenland), 6 (© sonya etchison), 7 (© Beata
Becla), 8 (© Stephen Mcsweeny), 9 (© Kzenon), 10 (©
Jorg Hackemann), 11 (© Cherry-Merry), 12 (© Lynne
Carpenter), 13 (© Monkey Business Images), 18 (©
AISPIX), 24 (© JustASC), 26 (© Monkey Business Images),
27 (© cappi thompson), 29 (© Zdenek Krchak).

Cover photograph of women running a race
reproduced with permission of Corbis (© Aflo).

We would like to thank Victoria Gray for her invaluable
help in the preparation of this book.

Every effort has been made to contact copyright
holders of material reproduced in this book. Any
omissions will be rectified in subsequent printings if
notice is given to the publisher.

Contents

Some words are shown in bold, **like this**. You can find out what they mean by looking in the glossary.

Let's Get Moving!

Have you ever heard that exercise is good for you? Well, it's true! Exercise keeps your bones strong, your heart pumping, and your muscles working well.

It can also make you feel happier and give you more energy.

BY THE NUMBERS
Kids should get at least 60 minutes of exercise every day.

It's time to get up and start moving!

What Is Stamina?

There are five different parts of fitness. They are **stamina**, flexibility, strength, speed, and **coordination**. Stamina is your staying power. The more stamina you have, the longer you can run and play without getting tired.

Building up your stamina will help you to run farther.

 When you have more stamina, you will be able to ride a bike farther, too.

When you improve your stamina, your heart pumps more easily and your lungs hold more air. This makes breathing easier—even when you are running.

Be Safe!

Exercise is a lot of fun, but it is more important to be safe. Always **warm up** before doing an **intense** activity. A good warm-up can be a nice, slow jog and some simple stretching exercises.

BY THE NUMBERS
Kids should warm up and cool down for 15 minutes before and after each exercise session.

There are many different stretches you can do to warm up your body.

Even if you are tired after exercise, don't just sit down. This makes your muscles sore and stiff. Instead, do a **cool-down** by stretching, jogging gently, or walking slowly for a while.

 You can keep your body safe by slowing down after you exercise, instead of stopping suddenly.

Drink Up!

Exercise makes you hot. Your body **sweats** to keep you cool. You have to drink lots of water to make up for the water you lose through sweat. This helps you to stay **hydrated**, which means there is enough water in your body for it to work properly.

Sweating helps to cool your body down.

Also remember that when the weather is warmer, you need more water.

You need to drink plenty of water when you exercise.

BY THE NUMBERS
Water makes up about 60 percent of your body weight.

Keep Walking!

Walking is the easiest way to build **stamina**. You can do it anytime or anywhere. Try to fit more walking into your daily life.

Does your mom or dad drive you to school? If it is safe, try walking together instead.

You can try walking at different speeds. Start off slowly and then see how quickly you can walk.

MINI CHALLENGE BOX

How long does it take to walk around your backyard or neighborhood? If you have a watch, time yourself. The next day, see if you can walk for two minutes longer than the first day. Continue to add two minutes each day until you reach 30 minutes or more.

Ask an adult which places you can walk to safely. Your friends might want to go with you.

Jumping Jacks

Jumping jacks are a great way to exercise and help you to build **stamina**. When you do a jumping jack, use your arms and legs to make your body into the letter X. Then bring your arms and legs together to form the letter I.

Go back and forth between being an X and being an I.

MINI CHALLENGE BOX

Try to do jumping jacks for the time it takes to listen to your favorite song. Then, try to do jumping jacks throughout two of your favorite songs.

1

2

15

Jumping Rope

Jumping rope is a great way to build **stamina**. Once you get the hang of it, it is fun and easy to do. When you begin to jump rope, stand with your feet slightly apart.

Hold the rope handles in each hand and keep the rope behind you, so that it rests at your heels. Use your wrists, not your arms, to swing the rope over your head. Each time the rope passes in front of you, jump!

MINI CHALLENGE BOX

When you jump rope, you stay in one spot and jump up and down. See if you can do skip jumps by moving forward as you jump.

Jump Rope Rhymes

Saying rhymes while you jump rope makes it even more fun and can help you to keep jumping for longer. Try these two rhymes:

Cinderella in her hat
Went back home to meet a cat
Made a mistake and met a snake
How many doctors did it take?
1...2...3...

MINI CHALLENGE BOX

Count until you miss a jump. See if you can get as high as 25.

When I was three, I banged my knee,
When I was four, I shut the door,
When I was five, I learned to jive,
When I was six, I picked up sticks...

MINI CHALLENGE BOX
Try to keep making up rhymes for each age until you make a mistake.

Make an Obstacle Course

An obstacle course is great exercise and also lots of fun. You can build one with whatever you have in your backyard. Maybe you could roll up beach towels and jump over them? Perfect!

You could also try crawling under some folding chairs or jumping through hula-hoops! If you don't have a backyard, you might be able to set up a course in a park or at a friend's house.

MINI CHALLENGE BOX

Invite friends over to see who can complete the obstacle course the fastest!

You could
try jumping
as fast as you
can from hoop
to hoop.

You could try doing 10
push-ups on a mat.

Hit the Hills

Is there a giant hill in your neighborhood that you can run up? Run up it as fast as you can, then roll down all the way to the bottom. Try to go up and down five times without taking a break.

If rolling down a hill isn't your thing, try running down!

MINI CHALLENGE BOX

Can't find a hill but have a set of stairs? Try climbing up and down those instead!

1

2

Be careful not to crash into anyone or anything when you roll down.

23

Ready, Set, Run!

To really test your **stamina**, try running. Like walking, you can do it anywhere. Start off by going slowly. Once you feel stronger, you can run for a little longer and run faster.

 Some places have running tracks you can use. People run along in their own lanes.

MINI CHALLENGE BOX

Using a stopwatch, try running for 10 minutes without stopping. Go at a nice, steady speed. Eventually, build up to running for 30 minutes without a break.

You can ask a friend with a stopwatch to let you know when to stop running.

Eating Well

Eating healthy food is also an important part of building **stamina**. Eating foods such as fruits and vegetables, along with whole grains and **protein** (such as bread and peanut butter), gives you energy to move. Eating food with too much sugar, such as cakes and cookies, makes you weaker.

There are lots of different fruits and vegetables you can try.

Fresh fruits are natural foods, and they can taste great with cereal.

Also remember that the more natural the food (the kind that grows on trees or in the ground), the better it is to eat. Try to only eat **processed** foods in small amounts.

Big Challenge

Deciding to run a marathon (26.2 miles, or 42.2 kilometers) may seem like an impossible goal at the moment. But if you keep practicing and **increasing** your **stamina**, you could run a marathon one day. It takes a lot of running, eating the right foods, and taking time for rest in between training.

Haile Gebrselassie (on the right) has won many marathons and received gold medals for running in the Olympics.

Keep working hard, and one day you could run a marathon!

Glossary

cool-down last part of a workout when the body is allowed to slow down

coordination ability to get different parts of the body to work well together

hydrated when a person has enough water in his or her body to stay healthy

increase become larger in size, strength, or number

intense of an extreme kind; very hard to keep doing

processed food that has been changed or had things added to it to make it last longer

protein substance in some foods that gives the body energy and helps it grow

stamina power to keep going or keep doing something

sweat release water through your skin

warm up do gentle exercises at the beginning of a workout

Find Out More

Books

Bodden, Valerie. *Running* (Active Sports).
  Mankato, Minn.: Creative Education, 2009.

Schaefer, A. R. *Exercise* (Health and Fitness).
  Chicago: Heinemann Library, 2010.

Senker, Cath. *Healthy Eating* (Healthy Choices).
  New York: PowerKids, 2008.

Websites

kidshealth.org/kid
Find out more about exercise, nutrition, and how
to stay healthy on this website.

www.kidsrunning.com
This website focuses on running.

www.letsmove.gov
This website encourages young people to
get moving.

Index